STECK-VAUGHN

# Comprehension Skills

# FACTS

## LEVEL
## F

Linda Ward Beech
Tara McCarthy
Donna Townsend

STECK-VAUGHN
COMPANY
A Subsidiary of National Education Corporation

| | |
|---|---|
| *Executive Editor:* | Diane Sharpe |
| *Project Editor:* | Melinda Veatch |
| *Senior Editor:* | Anne Rose Souby |
| *Design Coordinator:* | Sharon Golden |
| *Project Design:* | Howard Adkins Communications |
| *Cover Illustration:* | Rhonda Childress |
| *Photographs:* | ©Wally Eberhart / TSW / Click – Chicago |

ISBN 0-8114-7855-6

6 7 8 9 0 VP 00 99 98

Facts are things like names, dates, and places. In this book you will practice finding facts.

Sometimes you may notice more facts when you go on a trip away from home. Then you may see unusual facts all around you. What facts can you see in the picture on this page?

# What Are Facts?

Facts are sometimes called details. They are small pieces of information. Facts can appear in true stories, such as those in the newspaper. They can also appear in legends and other stories that people make up.

## How to Read for Facts

You can find facts by asking yourself questions. Ask *who*, and your answer will be a fact about a person. Ask *what*, and your answer will be a fact about a thing. Ask *where*, and your answer will be a fact about a place. Ask *when*, and your answer will be a fact about a time. Ask *how many* or *how much*, and your answer will be a fact about a number or an amount.

## Try It!

Read this story and look for facts as you read. Ask yourself *when* and *who*.

◆

### The First Airplane Flight

Wilbur and Orville Wright read everything they could find about flying machines. They began building their own airplane in 1899. They carefully tested every part of the airplane. Finally on a cold, windy day in December 1903, they flew their plane for the first time. Orville was the pilot as the plane lifted into the air. It stayed in the air for only 12 seconds and traveled just 120 feet the first time. After three more tries that same day, the plane's longest trip was almost a full minute and over 850 feet.

Did you find these facts when you read the paragraph? Write the facts on the lines below.

◆ When did the Wrights fly for the first time?

*Fact*: _____

◆ Who was the pilot?

*Fact*: _____

**To check your answers, turn to page 62.**

# *Practice Finding Facts*

Below are some practice questions. The first two are already answered. Answer the third one on your own.

___*C*___ **1.** How long was the plane's longest trip?

    **A.** 120 feet     **C.** 850 feet

    **B.** 85 feet     **D.** 12 feet

Look at the question and answers again. *How long* is asking for a number. There are many numbers in the paragraph, but you are looking for one that describes the plane's longest trip. Read the paragraph until you find the words *longest trip*. You should find this sentence: "After three more tries that same day, the plane's longest trip was almost a full minute and over 850 feet." So **c** is the correct answer. Answer **A** is also a fact from the story, but it describes the first trip, not the longest one.

___*D*___ **2.** The Wright brothers first flew their plane in

    **A.** summer     **C.** fall

    **B.** spring     **D.** winter

Look at the question. The first answer you might think of is a place. But the possible answers are seasons. Search the story for words about seasons or time of year. You should find this sentence: "Finally on a cold, windy day in December 1903, they flew their plane for the first time." The correct answer is *winter*. The answer uses different words, but the fact is the same.

Now it's your turn to practice. Answer the next question by writing the letter of the correct answer on the line.

_____ **3.** The Wrights first started working on their airplane in

    **A.** 1903     **C.** 1908

    **B.** 1899     **D.** 1809

**To check your answer, turn to page 62.**

# Using What You Know

Read the following question words and facts that answer the questions. Ask yourself the questions. Then write facts about yourself on the lines.

### Who?
Mary Lou Retton won five medals at the Olympics.
Abraham Lincoln was president during the Civil War.

◆ My name is _____.

### What?
The game ended in a tie.
The crowd ran onto the field.

◆ My favorite song is _____.

### Where?
The bus stops on Main Street.
The Amazon River flows through Brazil.

◆ I live in the city of _____.

### When?
School used to begin after Labor Day.
Columbus discovered the New World in 1492.

◆ I was born on _____, 19 ____.

### How Many?/How Much?
The team lost 14 of their 16 games.
A panda eats 45 pounds of bamboo a day.

◆ There are ____ students in my class.

# *How to Use This Book*

In this book you will read 25 stories. Each story has two parts. Read the first part, then answer five questions about it. Then read the second part and answer the next five questions.

When you finish reading each story and answering the questions about it, check your answers by looking at pages 59 through 61. Write the number of correct answers in the score box at the top of the page. After you finish all the stories, turn to pages 56 through 58 and work through "Think and Apply."

## *Remember*

This book asks questions about facts in stories. When you answer the questions, use the facts in the story. You may already know some facts about the subject, but the story will have the answers you need for the questions.

## *Hints for Better Reading*

◆ Look for facts while you are reading the stories. Notice the names of people, animals, and things. Look for places, dates, and times.

◆ Read each question carefully. Think about the facts you need to answer the question. Try to find a sentence in the story that has some of the same words as the question.

◆ Try to remember the facts you read in the story. If you can't remember, look back at the story.

## *Challenge Yourself*

Try this special challenge. Read each story. Cover the story with a sheet of paper, and try to remember the facts. Answer the questions without looking back at the story.

Birds have always been a problem for farmers. They like to eat the seeds in farmers' fields. As soon as a farmer plants seeds, the birds arrive for dinner. Often these birds are crows.

Farmers try to get rid of their unwanted visitors by making scarecrows. A scarecrow is supposed to scare away crows and other birds. The first scarecrows were made hundreds of years ago. They were sticks stuck in the ground with big rags tied to the top. When the wind blew, the rags flapped and frightened the birds.

As time went on, farmers began making better scarecrows. They nailed a second stick across the top of the one in the ground. Now the scarecrows had arms and could wear old shirts. When farmers stuffed the shirts with straw, the scarecrows began to look like real people. Some even had faces.

_____ **1.** Birds like to eat
    **A.** fields     **C.** worms
    **B.** seeds     **D.** sticks

_____ **2.** A scarecrow is supposed to scare away
    **A.** gardens     **C.** birds
    **B.** seeds     **D.** sticks

_____ **3.** The first scarecrows were made from sticks and
    **A.** rags     **C.** rugs
    **B.** plants     **D.** hats

_____ **4.** Later, farmers filled scarecrows with
    **A.** cotton     **C.** straw
    **B.** air     **D.** string

_____ **5.** Scarecrows flapped because of the
    **A.** arms     **C.** birds
    **B.** noise     **D.** wind

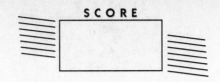

When farmers began using modern machines, they didn't need scarecrows anymore. The new farm machines were big and made a lot of noise. They scared the birds away quite well.

In the 1960s people became interested in folk art such as scarecrows. Suddenly scarecrows were popular again. People wanted them for their yards and vegetable gardens. Even people in cities bought scarecrows for their porches.

Today, some artists make scarecrows to sell. They use natural materials such as sticks and straw for the bodies. However, these new scarecrows are often dressed in fancy clothes. Some wear sunglasses, belts, or scarves. Lady scarecrows may have beads, flowers, and purses.

_____ 6. People didn't need scarecrows because they had
   A. clothes          C. workers
   B. machines         D. crows

_____ 7. In the 1960s people thought that scarecrows were
   A. folk art         C. farm workers
   B. sunglasses       D. fine art

_____ 8. People put scarecrows on porches and in
   A. machines         C. yards
   B. cities           D. parks

_____ 9. Today, some artists make scarecrows for
   A. sale             C. sail
   B. beads            D. style

_____ 10. Lady scarecrows sometimes have beads, flowers, and
   A. ties             C. pins
   B. shoes            D. purses

Basketball is the only major sport that is a totally American game. Jim Naismith started it all. During the 1880s Naismith taught athletics at a college in Massachusetts.

In the fall Naismith's students spent long, exciting hours on the football field. But when winter came, the students moved indoors and did exercises. Most students soon grew bored. They kept asking for an indoor game that was as exciting as football.

Naismith began to think about a new kind of ball game that could be played safely in a small gym. He decided that players wouldn't use bats or run while holding the ball. Players would use only their hands to pass or throw the ball to other players. Naismith still had one big question. How would players score points? He went to the college storeroom and pulled out two peach baskets!

_____ **1.** Jim Naismith was a teacher of
   **A.** history          **C.** athletics
   **B.** science          **D.** safety

_____ **2.** The students wanted an indoor
   **A.** game            **C.** exercise
   **B.** gym             **D.** coach

_____ **3.** In the new game, players would not use
   **A.** hands           **C.** bats
   **B.** goals           **D.** teams

_____ **4.** Players would pass or
   **A.** hit the ball    **C.** punch the ball
   **B.** throw the ball  **D.** kick the ball

_____ **5.** Naismith had a question about how players would
   **A.** find peach baskets   **C.** stay safe
   **B.** run with the ball    **D.** score points

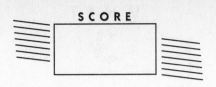
There was a balcony all around the gym. It was exactly ten feet above the floor. Naismith hung one peach basket on the balcony at each end of the gym. Then he divided the class into two teams of nine players each. The first basketball game began when he threw a soccer ball up between the team captains.

The players dashed up and down the gym. They yelled with excitement as they tried to throw the ball into the peach baskets. The game stopped for a while when one player finally sank the ball. Someone climbed a ladder to get it out. After all, there is no hole in the bottom of a peach basket! But that was the only pause in this first basketball game. The final score was 1–0.

As basketball became popular at other colleges, teams made up their own rules. However, a set of rules was developed within a few years. A special ball and an open hoop took the place of the soccer ball and peach baskets. The game of basketball had begun.

_____ **6.** The baskets were at a height of ten feet because of the
    **A.** floor      **C.** peaches
    **B.** balcony      **D.** ball

_____ **7.** Naismith's basketball teams were composed of
    **A.** nine players      **C.** fifty players
    **B.** thirty players      **D.** five players

_____ **8.** For a while the game was played with a
    **A.** basketball      **C.** football
    **B.** soccer ball      **D.** baseball

_____ **9.** The first baskets were
    **A.** closed at the bottom      **C.** open at the bottom
    **B.** made from ladders      **D.** filled with peaches

_____ **10.** For the first few years, basketball teams used
    **A.** Naismith's rules      **C.** their own rules
    **B.** today's rules      **D.** no rules

As early as 20,000 years ago, people painted pictures on the walls of caves. Many of the paintings were later found by people exploring the caves. Some are in places that can be reached only on hands and knees.

In 1879 a man and his daughter went into one of these caves in northern Spain. The man held a lighted candle as they made their way deep into the darkness. Suddenly his daughter shouted, "Toros! Toros!" ("Bulls! Bulls!") He looked up to see paintings of bison, or buffalo, on the cave's walls. The girl had found what are now known as the Altamira paintings. They are the most famous cave paintings in the world.

_____ 1. People painted on the walls of caves as early as
A. 30,000 years ago    C. 2,000 years ago
B. 20,000 years ago    D. 10,000 years ago

_____ 2. Some paintings can be reached only by using
A. a car              C. a train or bus
B. a rope             D. hands and knees

_____ 3. The Altamira paintings were found in
A. 1879              C. 89
B. 1789              D. 789

_____ 4. To find his way, the man used
A. a flashlight      C. a candle
B. a string          D. radar

_____ 5. The girl saw paintings of
A. bison             C. caves
B. horses            D. people

The people who had painted these remarkable pictures had worked deep inside the cave where there is no light. Yet they had painted many exact details of the animals' bodies. Experts think that they burned fat in stone lamps to light their work. They also think that the painters may have dragged the animals they painted into the caves.

No one knows why the artists went to so much trouble. But many people think that the paintings were part of a ceremony to bring good luck before a big hunt. The paintings show many wounded or dying animals. Others are shown swimming in a river where they would have been easy to catch.

_____ **6.** The caves where the artists worked were
    **A.** peaceful     **C.** dark
    **B.** windy     **D.** comfortable

_____ **7.** Many details in the paintings are
    **A.** sketchy     **C.** very faded
    **B.** exact     **D.** too large

_____ **8.** To help them paint details, the artists used
    **A.** sketches     **C.** small brushes
    **B.** strong colors     **D.** animals as models

_____ **9.** Perhaps the artists felt that painting helped them to
    **A.** farm     **C.** hunt
    **B.** sleep     **D.** swim

_____ **10.** In the paintings the animals appear
    **A.** weak     **C.** wild
    **B.** strong     **D.** hungry

People can learn history from cookbooks. Old cookbooks tell what foods people ate long ago. The books may also tell about eating customs.

One large collection of cookbooks is in Washington, D.C. It is part of the Library of Congress. This library belongs to the people of the United States. There are four thousand cookbooks in its collection. Most of them are very old and rare. Some are one of a kind.

The oldest cookbook at this library was written in 1475. It was written in Latin. It has twelve recipes for cooking fish. It also tells how to make many vegetable dishes. The famous Italian artist Leonardo da Vinci might have used this book. He did not eat meat.

---

_____ **1.** One thing people can learn from a cookbook is
- **A.** vegetables
- **C.** history
- **B.** reading
- **D.** science

_____ **2.** Cookbooks are records of people's foods and
- **A.** customs
- **C.** materials
- **B.** clothes
- **D.** collections

_____ **3.** The Library of Congress is in
- **A.** Italy
- **C.** Europe
- **B.** Latin
- **D.** Washington, D.C.

_____ **4.** The oldest cookbook in the library was written in
- **A.** 1475
- **C.** 1986
- **B.** 1745
- **D.** 1400

_____ **5.** This cookbook has twelve recipes for
- **A.** meat
- **C.** stew
- **B.** soup
- **D.** fish

The cookbooks at the Library of Congress trace cooking for five hundred years. The oldest cookbooks show that food wasn't as important to people as it is now. Long ago, eating was just something that people did in order to live. Later, people began to think of food as something to enjoy. Recipes became fancier. Food took more time to prepare.

Cookbooks from the 1700s show that people began to care more about how they served meals. These cookbooks have pages on how to fold napkins. They also show how to carve a goose or peel an orange.

Who uses these old cookbooks today? Suppose you were writing a story about the 1600s. You might want information on what people ate then. Or suppose you were a scientist studying a certain fruit. You might want to know when that fruit was first used. Old cookbooks are a record of the past.

_____

_____ **6.** Long ago, people just ate to stay
    **A.** full              **c.** sick
    **B.** alive           **D.** home

_____ **7.** In time, people thought of food as
    **A.** something to do    **c.** something to learn
    **B.** something to enjoy   **D.** something to happen

_____ **8.** As recipes became fancier, food took longer to
    **A.** eat              **c.** prepare
    **B.** write           **D.** serve

_____ **9.** In the 1700s cookbooks told how to
    **A.** wash napkins      **c.** fold chairs
    **B.** fold napkins       **D.** set tables

_____ **10.** Writers and scientists of today use old cookbooks for
    **A.** review          **c.** cooking
    **B.** imagination     **D.** information

Toronto has the world's largest shopping mall under the ground. It has more than one thousand shops and services. They are joined by miles of tunnels and sidewalks.

These tunnels and sidewalks also join 35 high-rise buildings. To get to the underground mall, shoppers go in one of the buildings and ride the elevator down. People can also take the subway to other parts of the city.

The city-under-the-city is always a pleasant place to walk. That's because the temperature is controlled. Outside, winter may be cold or summer may be hot. But deep down in the mall, the temperature stays the same all year round.

_____ 1. The largest underground mall is in
A. City Hall          C. Toronto
B. New York          D. an office building

_____ 2. In the shopping mall, there are more than one thousand
A. tunnels and sidewalks   C. business workers
B. shops and services      D. underground trains

_____ 3. The tunnels and sidewalks connect
A. thousands of tourists   C. cities in Canada
B. all parts of Toronto    D. 35 buildings

_____ 4. To get to other parts of Toronto, people take
A. tunnels          C. subways
B. sidewalks        D. elevators

_____ 5. The mall temperature is always
A. different        C. outside
B. the same         D. interesting

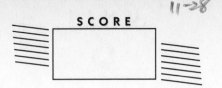
A city underground might be dark and gloomy. But Toronto's underground city is not that way at all. There are many bright lights. Shops are trimmed with polished metal and gleaming glass. Parts of the mall are on three levels. The levels are joined by stairs and elevators. Flowers and trees grow along the sidewalks.

The underground mall has more than shops. It has paintings and other works of art. It has theaters that give plays and concerts.

The city-under-the-city was so popular that Toronto business people began to worry! They wanted visitors to see Toronto at street level, too. So an aboveground mall was built at Eaton Centre. It has three hundred stores, several movie houses, and many restaurants.

_____ 6. The underground mall is
    A. gloomy        C. empty
    B. dark          D. bright

_____ 7. In the underground mall, you can shop and
    A. go to concerts        C. take art classes
    B. see Eaton Centre      D. buy glass

_____ 8. To get to different levels of the mall, you can use
    A. subways        C. sidewalks
    B. stairways        D. areas

_____ 9. The Eaton Centre mall is
    A. under the ground      C. above the buildings
    B. at street level        D. outside the city

_____ 10. Eaton Centre was built because
    A. a mall was needed      C. businesses wanted it
    B. stores were needed     D. Toronto was popular

The organ starts, and its music fills the air. The horses slowly begin to move. Riders hold tightly as their colorful horses go up and down and around and around. These riders are on a carousel. *Carousel* is another word for *merry-go-round.*

Carousels have a long history. In the 1400s soldiers in France liked to play a ball game on horseback. The soldiers had to throw and catch while their horses were moving. The French invented a way to help the soldiers practice for the game.

This invention was the first carousel. It was different from modern carousels. The biggest difference was that the horses were real! They turned the carousel as they moved in a circle. Years later, people began using carousels for fun. By the 1800s, carousel horses were no longer real. Carousels were run by motors.

_____ 1. *Merry-go-round* is another word for
    **A.** ferris wheel     **C.** roller coaster
    **B.** moving horse     **D.** carousel

_____ 2. The music for carousels comes from
    **A.** riders     **C.** pianos
    **B.** organs     **D.** radios

_____ 3. The first carousel was made to help players
    **A.** fight wars     **C.** ride horses
    **B.** invent tricks     **D.** practice skills

_____ 4. The horses on the first carousels were
    **A.** real     **C.** painted
    **B.** wood     **D.** motors

_____ 5. The first people to use a carousel were
    **A.** inventors     **C.** soldiers
    **B.** sailors     **D.** children

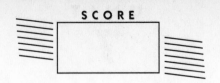

Once there were ten thousand merry-go-rounds in the United States. Most were made in Pennsylvania and New York. Workers carved and painted the carousel horses. Some horses had fine saddles and roses around their necks. Others had a wild look in their shiny glass eyes. No two horses were the same.

Today there are fewer than three hundred merry-go-rounds in the country. No one makes them anymore. Their time has passed.

The nation's oldest merry-go-round is in Oak Bluffs, Massachusetts. This carousel is called the Flying Horses. It was built around 1880. Riders on the Flying Horses can have some extra fun. As the merry-go-round spins, they try to grab rings from a post on the wall. The person who gets the most rings is the winner. The reward is a free ride.

_____ **6.** No two carousel horses were
    **A.** bright         **C.** carved
    **B.** wild          **D.** alike

_____ **7.** One state where carousels were made was
    **A.** Massachusetts   **C.** France
    **B.** Pennsylvania     **D.** Oak Bluffs

_____ **8.** Carousels are no longer being
    **A.** ridden         **C.** made
    **B.** painted       **D.** used

_____ **9.** America's oldest carousel is called the
    **A.** Oak Bluffs     **C.** Fighting Horses
    **B.** Flying Horses   **D.** New York

_____ **10.** A free ride on this merry-go-round is given as a
    **A.** prize          **C.** ring
    **B.** horse        **D.** win

Giant sequoia trees grow near the coast of northern California. Sequoia trees are also called redwoods. For many years experts thought that these tall trees were the oldest living trees on earth. In 1892 one of the trees was cut down. Scientists counted the growth rings in the tree to find out its age. They discovered that the tree was indeed old. It had lived for about 3,212 years. Today experts know that the redwood trees average about 3,500 years in age.

Redwood trees have straight trunks and branches that seem to brush against the sky. One redwood, named "General Sherman," is the largest living thing in the world. It is 272 feet tall.

_____ 1. Redwood trees are also called
  A. oak trees      C. cedars
  B. elm trees      D. sequoias

_____ 2. Experts once thought the redwoods were the
  A. youngest trees      C. tallest trees
  B. oldest trees      D. prettiest trees

_____ 3. To find out the age of a tree, scientists count its
  A. rings      C. trunks
  B. leaves      D. branches

_____ 4. In 1892 a redwood was discovered to be
  A. 212 years old      C. 3,212 years old
  B. 215 years old      D. 2,012 years old

_____ 5. "General Sherman" is
  A. 272 feet tall      C. 727 feet tall
  B. 288 feet tall      D. 242 feet tall

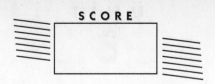

In 1953 scientists became interested in another type of tree. They had discovered some very old bristlecone pines in Nevada. At heights of only 20 to 60 feet, these pines were not as grand as the redwoods. But the experts began to wonder if they were older.

In 1957 they found a pine over 4,000 years old. Their theory had been correct. Further study turned up even older trees. One of these trees, "Methuselah," is the oldest living tree in the world. It is 4,700 years old. But even though the pines are older, they may not live as long as the redwoods. This is because the redwoods have a longer life span.

_____ **6.** In 1953 scientists became interested in another
   **A.** state          **C.** pine cone
   **B.** wildflower      **D.** type of tree

_____ **7.** Experts discovered some pine trees that were
   **A.** dying          **C.** very old
   **B.** tall           **D.** useful

_____ **8.** Compared to redwoods, pine trees are not as
   **A.** tall           **C.** healthy
   **B.** rough          **D.** green

_____ **9.** The oldest living tree in the world is
   **A.** a redwood      **C.** Methuselah
   **B.** a sequoia      **D.** General Sherman

_____ **10.** Although the pines are older, the redwoods will
   **A.** die soon       **C.** live longer
   **B.** live forever   **D.** stay small

There are all kinds of contests. Have you ever heard of the Apple Seed Popping Contest? It's held on the first weekend in October in Lincoln, Nebraska. How does it work? Line up with everybody else. Take a fresh apple, and squeeze it hard in your fist. If your apple seeds pop the farthest, you're a winner!

Do you like food contests? Every August in Fulton, Kentucky, there's a banana contest. If you eat the most bananas within a set time, you win some more bananas. If you like milk, go to Los Angeles, California, in September. Sign up for the Milk Drinking Contest. If you win, you get a ribbon.

In Albany, Oregon, anyone between the ages of five and twelve can enter the Bubble Gum Blowing Contest. You'll win some books if you blow the first bubble, the biggest bubble, or the bubble that lasts the longest.

_____ 1. The Apple Seed Popping Contest is held in
   A. California        C. August
   B. October          D. Albany

_____ 2. To win the Apple Seed Popping Contest, you must
   A. be under sixteen    C. pop seeds the farthest
   B. line up the seeds   D. squeeze the fresh apple

_____ 3. The winner of the banana contest gets
   A. a set time        C. more bananas
   B. a ribbon          D. a trip to Fulton

_____ 4. People who like milk could sign up for a contest in
   A. Los Angeles       C. Oregon
   B. Nebraska          D. Kentucky

_____ 5. The person who blows the biggest bubble wins
   A. gum               C. books
   B. food              D. bikes

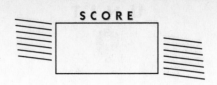
Some contests require a special animal. In May bring your chicken to the Chicken Flying Meet in Rio Grande, Ohio. Put your chicken on the launch pad. At the signal, give it a little push. If your chicken flies the farthest, you win a cash prize.

People fourteen and under can enter the Greasy Pig Scramble in Dotham, Alabama. The pigs are greased with peanut oil. You have to catch the greasy pig and hold on to it until it crosses the finish line. If you win, you get the pig.

If you have a pet crab, you can enter it in the World Championship Crab Race in California. The International Frog Jumping and Racing Contest is held in Louisiana. Winners of both contests get medals. Petaluma, California, holds an Ugly Dog Contest. The winners receive medals and are invited to come back next year for the Ugliest Dog Contest.

_____ **6.** In some contests, you need a pet that is
   **A.** slow         **C.** afraid
   **B.** prized        **D.** unusual

_____ **7.** The Chicken Flying Meet is in
   **A.** Ohio         **C.** California
   **B.** Alabama      **D.** Louisiana

_____ **8.** In the Dotham, Alabama, contest you have to
   **A.** use peanuts  **C.** count pigs
   **B.** hold on      **D.** push chickens

_____ **9.** Louisiana has a special contest for
   **A.** frogs        **C.** crabs
   **B.** dogs         **D.** pigs

_____ **10.** The Ugliest Dog Contest is for dogs that
   **A.** are not strange   **C.** won the year before
   **B.** live in Ohio      **D.** like to get medals

When he was a child, Ray Ewry became ill with a fever. His doctors told him that he had polio. Polio is a disease that causes people to become paralyzed. Ray gradually got better, but he found that his legs had been weakened by his illness. The doctors thought that leg exercises might help him regain his strength. But they told Ray that he probably would never be able to walk and run as he once had.

For the next few years, Ray exercised daily. He did everything his doctors had recommended and more. After a while he could tell that his hard work was paying off. His legs became stronger and stronger. He even began to take part in track and field events.

_____ **1.** The disease that Ray Ewry had was
- **A.** the measles
- **B.** chicken pox
- **C.** polio
- **D.** tuberculosis

_____ **2.** When he got better, Ray found that his legs were
- **A.** stronger
- **B.** weaker
- **C.** longer
- **D.** broken

_____ **3.** Doctors told Ray that he would not be able to
- **A.** sleep
- **B.** eat
- **C.** walk and run
- **D.** lift heavy things

_____ **4.** For the next few years, Ray exercised
- **A.** every two weeks
- **B.** once a month
- **C.** weekly
- **D.** daily

_____ **5.** Ray began to take part in
- **A.** track and field
- **B.** swimming
- **C.** football
- **D.** soccer

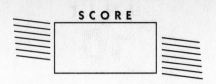

Soon Ray could jump higher and farther than most people. So he entered the Olympics in 1900 and signed up for three contests. He entered the standing high jump, the standing long jump, and the standing hop, step, and jump. He won gold medals, or first place, in all three events.

Ray repeated his amazing feat in 1904 and planned to try again in 1906. But before the next games, the hop, skip, and jump was dropped from the list of events. So Ray had to settle for only two gold medals in 1906 and two again in 1908. Ray had indeed overcome his illness. Today he holds the record for the most gold medals ever given to any one person.

---

**6.** Soon Ray became very
   **A.** shy           **C.** skilled
   **B.** tired         **D.** bored

**7.** In the 1900 Olympics, Ray entered
   **A.** jumping contests   **C.** pole vaulting
   **B.** running contests   **D.** five contests

**8.** In 1900 Ray won gold medals in
   **A.** one event      **C.** three events
   **B.** two events     **D.** four events

**9.** In the 1906 games, the hop, skip, and jump was
   **A.** held twice     **C.** won
   **B.** dropped      **D.** thrilling

**10.** Ray holds the record for the most
   **A.** jumps        **C.** gold medals
   **B.** events       **D.** Olympics

## The Turning Wheel

Once a poor student had to wander about the countryside. He had no money, and he had no home. One freezing night the student knocked at the door of a farmer's house. The farmer was an agreeable person who said, "Come in! You look very tired and hungry." The farmer gave the student supper, and the two began talking. The farmer asked whether the student could answer a question he was wondering about. He asked, "What is it that the gods are doing up in the sky tonight?" The student pondered for a long time but confessed that he didn't know the answer. "Never mind," said the farmer. "Maybe there is no answer."

The farmer gave the student a cozy room in which to sleep and a big breakfast the next morning. "Now," said the student, "I'll be on my way. But I will always be grateful to you for your kindness."

_____ **1.** The student had no
  **A.** friends　　　**C.** money
  **B.** sense　　　　**D.** family

_____ **2.** The farmer was
  **A.** wise　　　　**C.** tired
  **B.** cold　　　　**D.** friendly

_____ **3.** The student did not
  **A.** know the answer　**C.** go to sleep
  **B.** act intelligent　　**D.** eat enough

_____ **4.** The farmer gave the student
  **A.** a god　　　　**C.** a big breakfast
  **B.** some money　**D.** the answer

_____ **5.** The student thanked the farmer for his
  **A.** room　　　　**C.** kindness
  **B.** breakfast　　**D.** answer

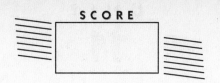
The student traveled on. He eventually found a good job as a teacher and purchased a home of his own. One day the teacher saw a very old fellow limping up the path. His hair was white and thin, and his clothes were ragged. The teacher invited the old man in. He fed the man, and as they talked, the younger man recognized the stranger as the farmer who assisted him long ago.

The teacher said, "Now I know the answer to the question you asked me. The gods were constructing a wheel that turns very, very slowly. Someday the person at the top will be at the bottom, and the person at the bottom will be at the top. And since we are all on the same wheel, my friend, you may live in my house in comfort all the days of your life."

_____ **6.** After a while the student
    **A.** became a farmer    **C.** lost his money
    **B.** became a teacher    **D.** limped up the path

_____ **7.** The teacher gave the older man
    **A.** a wheel        **C.** food to eat
    **B.** rags to wear    **D.** houses to own

_____ **8.** The teacher and the old man knew
    **A.** the farmer     **C.** the world
    **B.** an answer      **D.** each other

_____ **9.** The teacher thought the gods were
    **A.** being unfair     **C.** turning slowly
    **B.** building a wheel    **D.** asking questions

_____ **10.** In the end the old man had a
    **A.** life         **C.** home
    **B.** penny      **D.** comfort

In the 1880s William Frisbie and his sister were working hard at their pie business in Connecticut. She baked the pies. He took them to customers. The pies came in special metal plates called pie tins. Each tin had the words *Frisbie's Pies* on the bottom. The students at Yale University liked Frisbie pies. They liked Frisbie pie tins even better. They made up a game called Pie Tin Catch. With a flick of the wrist, they could send a pie tin flying. But people could get hurt if they were hit with a tin. So students yelled the warning "Frisbie!" as they tossed it.

In 1948 a man named William Morrison saw that Americans were fascinated by pictures and stories about strange space ships. They were called flying saucers. So Morrison designed a plastic toy in that shape. He called it a Pluto Platter. Soon Pluto Platters were flying all over beaches and parks.

_____  **1.** The Frisbies delivered
    **A.** bridges     **C.** businesses
    **B.** toys     **D.** pies

_____  **2.** The students at Yale liked
    **A.** studying     **C.** customers
    **B.** tests     **D.** pies

_____  **3.** Pie Tin Catch was a
    **A.** label     **C.** warning
    **B.** game     **D.** saucer

_____  **4.** In 1948 Americans were interested in
    **A.** toys     **C.** pies
    **B.** flying saucers     **D.** parks

_____  **5.** Morrison's toys were made of
    **A.** plastic     **C.** shapes
    **B.** Pluto     **D.** photos

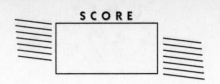

In 1955 Richard Knerr and Spud Mulligan started a toy company. They bought the rights to the Pluto Platter. But for a while, the Pluto Platter lost its popularity to another toy called the Hula Hoop. People all over America were spinning hoops instead of throwing Pluto Platters.

Richard Knerr found out about the old game called Frisbieing. He decided to give the Pluto Platter its original name. But he spelled it *Frisbee* by mistake. In the early 1960s, people got tired of Hula Hoops. They wanted to play with flying plastic saucers again. Today there are Frisbees that glow in the dark and cloth Frisbees that can be tucked in a pocket. Foam-rubber Frisbees are used indoors. The Frisbie pies may be forgotten, but Frisbees are here to stay.

_____ **6.** Knerr and Mulligan started a
    **A.** new game    **C.** toy company
    **B.** plate business    **D.** pie business

_____ **7.** The Hula Hoop was a special kind of
    **A.** dance    **C.** toy
    **B.** exercise    **D.** tin

_____ **8.** Knerr learned about
    **A.** college students    **C.** family names
    **B.** selling Frisbees    **D.** an old game

_____ **9.** In the 1960s people wanted
    **A.** to be indoors    **C.** bigger hoops
    **B.** flying toys    **D.** cloth Frisbees

_____ **10.** Foam-rubber Frisbees can be used in
    **A.** the house    **C.** the dark
    **B.** a pocket    **D.** plastic

It was a gray November day in 1963. A fishing boat rocked in the Atlantic Ocean off the southern coast of Iceland. Suddenly a great black cloud burst from the water. Loud noises rumbled from the ocean, too. The ship's captain sent out a radio call. Something very unusual was happening!

In the next three hours, scientists and reporters arrived at the scene. By now the cloud was twelve thousand feet high. Huge explosions sent ash, dust, and hot rocks into the air. The watchers could see something just under the water's surface.

By that night a new mountain had pushed itself up from the boiling sea. The mountain continued to rise during the next days. It also grew wider. A fiery island was growing in the Atlantic. It was caused by a volcano in the ocean.

---

_____ **1.** The fishing boat was off the coast of
    **A.** Ireland     **C.** Iceland
    **B.** Greenland     **D.** November

_____ **2.** The ship's captain used a
    **A.** radio     **C.** telephone
    **B.** light     **D.** surface

_____ **3.** The explosions sent up ash, dust, and hot
    **A.** food     **C.** ice
    **B.** rocks     **D.** fish

_____ **4.** The mountain grew into
    **A.** an island     **C.** a valley
    **B.** a nation     **D.** an iceberg

_____ **5.** The explosion came from
    **A.** an island     **C.** an earthquake
    **B.** a volcano     **D.** a fishing boat

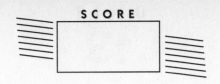
The new island continued to grow for two years. It finally stopped in August of 1965. It was 550 feet high. It was more than a mile long and about six miles around.

The people of Iceland named the new island Surtsey. This name comes from an old myth. In the story Surtur was a mighty fire giant. People thought that Surtsey was also a giant by the time it stopped growing.

Scientists are very interested in Surtsey. It is the first new island to appear in the North Atlantic in two hundred years. Scientists want to learn more about how this happened. They are also studying how plant life begins on a new island. Another thing scientists want to know is how long Surtsey will last. They wonder whether the island will be destroyed by the same volcano that created it.

_____ 6. The new island became quiet in
  A. 1956          C. the old story
  B. 1963          D. 1965

_____ 7. Surtur was a fire giant in an old
  A. tale          C. snow
  B. island        D. volcano

_____ 8. In the myth Surtur was
  A. cloudy        C. powerful
  B. weak          D. peaceful

_____ 9. Scientists are studying
  A. plant life    C. people
  B. dead fish     D. animal life

_____ 10. Scientists also want to know how long Surtsey will
  A. return        C. burn
  B. remain        D. flood

All over the country, many Americans are learning to "Dip for the Oyster," "Box the Gnat," and "Wring the Dishrag." These are special names for different movements in square dances.

A square-dance party may be called by many names. Such a party may be called a hog wrassle, a hoedown, a barndance, or a shindig. But all square dances are alike in certain ways. Four couples line up and face each other. A caller chants or sings directions. The dancers shuffle, glide, or run while people clap.

Pioneers in New England started these dances. As people moved westward and southward, new movements were added. In the Midwest, dancers created the "Grand Right and Left." In the far West, cowboys lifted their partners off the ground during "The Swing."

_____ **1.** The dance movements have special
- **A.** squares
- **B.** names
- **C.** shindigs
- **D.** boxes

_____ **2.** A hoedown is a kind of
- **A.** party
- **B.** sport
- **C.** step
- **D.** tool

_____ **3.** The caller gives
- **A.** parties
- **B.** directions
- **C.** squares
- **D.** barndances

_____ **4.** Square dancing started in
- **A.** the Far West
- **B.** the South
- **C.** New England
- **D.** the Midwest

_____ **5.** In "The Swing," men lifted their partners
- **A.** to the right
- **B.** to the left
- **C.** off the ground
- **D.** Grand Right and Left

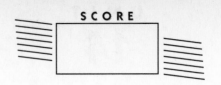
Square dancing comes from dances done long ago in England. People there did *country dances.* In one country dance, dancers formed a circle. This dance was called a round. Another country dance was the longways. In this one, two long lines of dancers faced one another. A popular longways is called the Virginia Reel.

Around the year 1900, square dancing was dying out. Dancers liked the new *couple dancing* better. But in the 1940s, people became interested in the songs and dances the pioneers enjoyed. Square dancing became popular again. The interest in square dancing is still growing. But it's not easy to learn some of those movements! Square-dance contests award ribbons or badges to the winners. So if you're invited to a hog wrassle, get ready for music, action, and fun.

_____ **6.** In a round
- **A.** a circle is formed
- **B.** a longways is danced
- **C.** Americans dance
- **D.** people dance in Virginia

_____ **7.** The Virginia Reel is a
- **A.** longways
- **B.** square
- **C.** couple dance
- **D.** new name

_____ **8.** Between 1900 and 1940, couple dancing became
- **A.** impossible
- **B.** popular
- **C.** a round
- **D.** a longways

_____ **9.** Square dancing started again when people became
- **A.** interested in history
- **B.** better Americans
- **C.** tired of couples
- **D.** buyers of clothing

_____ **10.** In a square-dance contest, people earn
- **A.** boots
- **B.** music
- **C.** difficult movements
- **D.** ribbons or badges

Ilse Bing was a photographer in the 1930s. She was one of the first photographers to use a camera to make works of art. Cameras had been around since the late 1800s. However, most photographers used them to take pictures of news events or famous people. Bing took photos of people who were dressed beautifully or oddly.

At about the same time, Laura Gilpin was working in the American Southwest. She took pictures as she hiked through the desert. One of Gilpin's most famous pictures is called *Shiprock, New Mexico*. It shows a gigantic rock standing alone in a valley. Gilpin made many of her prints on a special soft paper. The special paper made her prints look cloudy and gray, like old paintings. That's the way Gilpin wanted her work to look.

_____ **1.** Ilse Bing was one of the first
    **A.** cameras      **C.** art photographers
    **B.** photographs   **D.** news events

_____ **2.** Bing wanted to take photographs that were
    **A.** art      **C.** news
    **B.** famous   **D.** first

_____ **3.** *Shiprock, New Mexico* is a
    **A.** picture    **C.** valley
    **B.** desert    **D.** ship

_____ **4.** Laura Gilpin worked in
    **A.** the Southwest  **C.** the South
    **B.** Germany     **D.** the West

_____ **5.** Gilpin wanted her pictures to look like
    **A.** soft paper    **C.** old paintings
    **B.** other photos  **D.** gray clouds

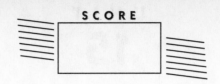
Ilse Bing chose subjects that were quite different from Gilpin's. She liked city life. She loved bright lights, big buildings, and constant movement. She took pictures in Germany and France. Then in 1941 she moved to New York City. Soon magazines were using her work.

Laura Gilpin stayed in the Southwest. She made photo landscapes in black and white on special paper. She could make a river look like a black snake, curving through the white desert sand.

When Gilpin died, she left thousands of striking photographs. Bing's collection may be just as large. Museums now treasure their work. Photographs by Bing and Gilpin are shown in cities all over the world.

_____ **6.** Ilse Bing took pictures of
  **A.** dresses      **C.** cities
  **B.** magazines    **D.** rivers

_____ **7.** Gilpin made black-and-white photo landscapes with
  **A.** desert sand      **C.** city life
  **B.** special paper    **D.** curving snakes

_____ **8.** In 1941 Ilse Bing moved to
  **A.** Germany        **C.** France
  **B.** the Southwest  **D.** New York City

_____ **9.** Museums now think that Bing's and Gilpin's work is
  **A.** small   **C.** valuable
  **B.** dull    **D.** worthless

_____ **10.** Photographs by Bing and Gilpin are shown
  **A.** only in Paris   **C.** only in the Southwest
  **B.** everywhere      **D.** in landscapes

Words like *light* and *natural* appear in large, bright letters across many cans and boxes of food. But these words, and others like them, sometimes give shoppers false ideas about the food inside. Even though laws require that all food labels give truthful information, this does not always happen.

The word *natural* has not been defined by the FDA, the agency in charge of food labels. So any food maker can use the word on a package. Even the worst junk food is certain to have something natural in it. So the makers of these foods can use the word *natural* on the package.

_____ **1.** By reading food labels, shoppers can
- **A.** get false ideas
- **B.** find bargains
- **C.** be truthful
- **D.** win prizes

_____ **2.** Laws require that food labels be
- **A.** bright
- **B.** natural
- **C.** printed
- **D.** truthful

_____ **3.** The word *natural* has not been
- **A.** defined
- **B.** used
- **C.** written
- **D.** understood

_____ **4.** The FDA is in charge of
- **A.** food pricing
- **B.** food labels
- **C.** shopping
- **D.** packaging

_____ **5.** All junk food contains something that is
- **A.** tasty
- **B.** nutritious
- **C.** natural
- **D.** sweet

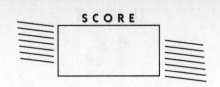
The word *light* might also confuse shoppers. Those who need to keep fat out of their diet might look for this word on foods. But because there is no strict definition, food makers might put *light* on food with a light color or food that is light in weight. Even less clear are labels that say *fat-free* or *salt-free.* Under the current rules, food makers can put a label with these words on foods that do, in fact, have small amounts of fat or salt.

Many people have written letters of complaint to the FDA. They want to know what is really in the food they eat. The FDA is responding. Soon labels will give information that tells the truth. In the meantime, read those labels carefully.

_____

_____ 6. The word *light* on food labels is often
    A. banned      C. truthful
    B. interesting      D. misunderstood

_____ 7. Food with the word *light* on the label might be
    A. lightweight      C. heavy
    B. juicy      D. sweet

_____ 8. Sometimes foods with labels that say *salt-free* are
    A. spicy      C. sweet
    B. salty      D. bitter

_____ 9. People have sent letters to the FDA with their
    A. praise      C. pictures
    B. complaints      D. labels

_____ 10. Until the rules are changed, you should read labels
    A. quickly      C. carefully
    B. aloud      D. rarely

How would you like to come home after a long day, open the door, and walk into an elephant? That's what you would do if you lived in Elephant House in Margate, New Jersey. The elephant-shaped house was built in 1881 by James Lafferty. Herbert Green built a chicken-shaped house in 1962.

Sarah Winchester tried to build a ghost-proof house in San Jose, California. Workers built fake chimneys, doors that open onto blank walls, and stairs that lead nowhere. Many rooms were torn down and then rebuilt in a new way to confuse the ghosts. It took 38 years to complete the house!

Some houses are built of strange materials. A house in Pigeon Cove, Massachusetts, is built from more than one hundred thousand newspapers. In Canada, George Plumb built a house entirely out of bottles.

_____ **1.** The elephant-shaped house was built in
  **A.** 1881         **C.** 1922
  **B.** 1884         **D.** 1962

_____ **2.** Green's house is shaped like
  **A.** a chicken     **C.** an elephant
  **B.** a door        **D.** a pigeon

_____ **3.** Sarah Winchester built a house in
  **A.** Massachusetts  **C.** New Jersey
  **B.** California      **D.** Oklahoma

_____ **4.** Winchester tried to build a house that was
  **A.** a castle       **C.** rebuilt
  **B.** fool-proof     **D.** ghost-proof

_____ **5.** George Plumb's house is built of
  **A.** newspapers     **C.** chimneys
  **B.** aluminum cans  **D.** bottles

Some homes stand for great wealth and power. The Palace of Alhambra in Spain is one of the most beautiful homes in the world. The man who built it loved water. A stream runs through all nine acres of the palace. In each room there is a small pool of sparkling water.

Wealthy Americans design dream houses, too. In 1895 Cornelius Vanderbilt moved into a house named the Breakers. He called it his summer cottage. It cost ten million dollars to build and has walls trimmed with gold. This "summer cottage" could hold sixty guests comfortably.

Dream houses don't have to be expensive. A man named Baldasera built a house with ninety rooms for about three hundred dollars by digging under the earth. Baldasera worked alone. He spent about forty years completing his underground house.

_____ **6.** The Palace of Alhambra covers
   **A.** forty years    **C.** ten million dollars
   **B.** nine acres    **D.** ninety rooms

_____ **7.** The builder of the Palace of Alhambra loved
   **A.** water    **C.** wealth and power
   **B.** chances to swim    **D.** pools with lights

_____ **8.** Vanderbilt designed the Breakers to be his summer
   **A.** museum    **C.** home
   **B.** camp    **D.** dream

_____ **9.** Baldasera built his home
   **A.** in Spain    **C.** without much money
   **B.** at the Breakers    **D.** in a mountain

_____ **10.** To build his house, Baldasera needed much
   **A.** help    **C.** time
   **B.** water    **D.** money

A dozen small turtles slide off a rock and slip into the pond. These turtles look as if an artist had painted them. Pale yellow stripes cross their upper shells, and a red border circles the edge. More red and yellow stripes are on the turtles' heads, and just behind each eye is another yellow spot.

These eastern painted turtles live in marshy areas, ponds, and slow-moving rivers. They like to be in places where rocks and fallen trees project from the water. The turtles like to climb out onto the rocks or dead trees to sleep in the warm sunlight. If something frightens them, they slide quickly into the water.

Eastern painted turtles keep regular schedules. They nap at certain times, and they eat at certain times. In the late morning and the late afternoon, the turtles search for food.

_____ **1.** Eastern painted turtles are mainly red and
  **A.** green          **C.** blue
  **B.** orange         **D.** yellow

_____ **2.** These turtles live near rivers that are
  **A.** deep           **C.** slow
  **B.** warm           **D.** fast

_____ **3.** The turtles like to sleep
  **A.** in the sunlight    **C.** inside trees
  **B.** under the water    **D.** while eating

_____ **4.** The turtles move quickly when they are
  **A.** hungry         **C.** sleepy
  **B.** certain        **D.** frightened

_____ **5.** In the late afternoon, the turtles
  **A.** climb on rocks     **C.** slide into the water
  **B.** search for food    **D.** go swimming

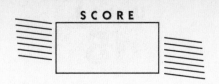
Painted turtles eat almost anything they can find in their water homes. They feed on plants, insects, crayfish, and snails. Since young turtles need to grow fast, they usually eat more animal food than older turtles do. When winter comes, the turtles dig into the underwater mud and sleep there until warm weather returns.

Once a year, in the early summer, the females crawl to dry land. There they dig nests and lay their eggs. In about ten weeks, the young turtles hatch, and the real battle for life begins. As the turtles creep toward the water, many of them are caught and eaten by hungry raccoons, snakes, and bullfrogs.

Some varieties of young eastern painted turtles stay in their nests all through their first summer, fall, and winter. When they come out the following spring, they are larger, stronger, and quicker. Then they have a better chance of escaping their enemies.

_____ **6.** To turtles, crayfish and snails are
  **A.** insects      **C.** enemies
  **B.** food       **D.** friends

_____ **7.** Animal food helps turtles
  **A.** grow quickly    **C.** eat more
  **B.** swim faster     **D.** sleep longer

_____ **8.** In the winter the turtles live
  **A.** close to water    **C.** under the mud
  **B.** on dry land     **D.** in warm homes

_____ **9.** Little turtles can be caught as they
  **A.** dig their nests    **C.** crawl toward water
  **B.** lay their eggs     **D.** hunt snakes

_____ **10.** Some varieties of turtles remain in their nests
  **A.** until they lay eggs   **C.** for about ten weeks
  **B.** to hide from raccoons   **D.** for almost a year

"What an ugly boy!" many people whispered when they saw Hans Christian Andersen. His hands and feet were gigantic. His eyes were tiny, and his nose was too big for such a thin face. He seemed clumsy as he clattered to school in his wooden shoes. Young Hans lived a sad life. His father was a poor shoemaker, and his mother was often ill. So the lonely boy created a make-believe world of his own, designing toy theaters and carving tiny figures to act in them.

In 1819, when Hans was fourteen, he made a big decision. He left his home and traveled across Denmark to the city of Copenhagen. "Here," declared Hans, "I will make my dream come true. I will become a famous actor." But it soon became evident that the dream would not come true at all. For three years Hans tried to find an acting job but had no luck. When he was seventeen, Hans sadly returned home.

_____  **1.** Hans Andersen's hands were
  **A.** small     **C.** gigantic
  **B.** thin     **D.** clumsy

_____  **2.** Andersen's father was
  **A.** lonely     **C.** ill
  **B.** poor     **D.** unkind

_____  **3.** Hans designed toy
  **A.** theaters     **C.** shoes
  **B.** books     **D.** plays

_____  **4.** In Copenhagen Hans could not find
  **A.** a perfect theater     **C.** a comfortable home
  **B.** an acting teacher     **D.** an acting job

_____  **5.** As he went home, Hans felt
  **A.** hopeful     **C.** famous
  **B.** sad     **D.** tired

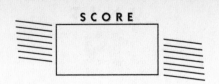
Hans went back to school and worked hard at his lessons. He kept a journal, which he filled with his dreams, thoughts, and ideas for stories. In his journal Hans told about an ugly bird that was laughed at by the ducklings in a farmyard. But the little bird was not a duck at all, and it grew into an elegant swan.

Hans graduated from school with a new dream of becoming a famous writer of novels and articles. He kept busy at his writing. But publishers would not buy his books or news stories, and it seemed that this dream, too, would never come true. By the time he was thirty, Hans was very poor indeed. He decided to try writing stories for children. Adults and children loved these stories! People of all ages still do.

Perhaps the Andersen story that people know best is "The Ugly Duckling." In a way it is the story of Andersen himself.

_____  6. During his school days, Hans
   A. studied birds    C. became famous
   B. wrote lessons    D. recorded his thoughts

_____  7. The ugly bird was really a
   A. swan      C. student
   B. duckling     D. child

_____  8. Andersen could not sell his
   A. dreams     C. novels
   B. publishers    D. ducks

_____  9. Andersen started to write children's stories when he was
   A. in school    C. famous
   B. thirty      D. on a farm

_____  10. "The Ugly Duckling" may really be about Andersen's own
   A. school     C. fame
   B. life       D. ways

In May of 1856, a strange cargo walked off a naval ship at Old Powder Horn, Texas. The cargo was 33 camels from Arabia. A man named Hadji Ali led the camels onto the dock. He was an Arab "camel conductor." At that time, few Americans had ever seen a camel. The animals were unfriendly. They spit, kicked, and snorted. Hadji Ali's job was to teach United States soldiers how to manage them.

Secretary of War Jefferson Davis brought the camels west to move supplies across the deserts. Mules, horses, and oxen were not always strong enough to make the trip. Camels were used for long desert voyages. They could go without water for many days. To find out how tough the camels really were, soldiers took 25 mules and 25 camels on a long, hard trip. The mules finally stumbled and fell. But the camels returned in good shape.

_____ **1.** The camels came to Texas on a
    **A.** truck         **C.** car
    **B.** train         **D.** ship

_____ **2.** Hadji Ali taught soldiers how to
    **A.** be conductors     **C.** make trips
    **B.** handle camels     **D.** fight wars

_____ **3.** Jefferson Davis wanted the camels to
    **A.** carry supplies     **C.** go without water
    **B.** climb ledges     **D.** work with mules

_____ **4.** Jefferson Davis was
    **A.** a ship captain     **C.** Secretary of the Army
    **B.** a soldier     **D.** Secretary of War

_____ **5.** The camels returned from the hard trip
    **A.** in fine shape     **C.** as tough as Davis
    **B.** on their knees     **D.** stumbling and falling

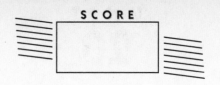
At first the camels were roped together in long lines. But when the lead camel tripped, all the other camels behind it tripped, too. Precious water was lost. The soldiers finally learned what Hadji Ali had told them. Camels will follow one another without being tied.

By 1861 the Civil War was sweeping the country. Confederate troops captured many Union Army camps in the West. They captured the camels, too. The soldiers did not know what to do with eighty camels. They used some to carry cotton to Mexico. But most of the camels were set free. They were just too hard to control. So the camels wandered alone in the desert. Once in a while, a surprised traveler would report seeing one. These reports died out after a few years, just as the camels did. As for Hadji Ali, he lived a long life in Arizona, where people called him Hi-Jolly.

_____ **6.** Water was spilled when
    **A.** soldiers cut ropes   **C.** water was found
    **B.** a camel stumbled   **D.** Hadji Ali left

_____ **7.** Camels will walk in a line without
    **A.** ropes           **C.** leaders
    **B.** cliffs           **D.** water

_____ **8.** The Confederate Army used camels to
    **A.** capture camps   **C.** build circuses
    **B.** trick traders     **D.** carry cotton

_____ **9.** After a few years, the camels
    **A.** chased travelers   **C.** went home
    **B.** went to Mexico   **D.** died out

_____ **10.** People in Arizona gave Hadji Ali
    **A.** a long life     **C.** a new name
    **B.** another camel   **D.** a good home

Many hundreds of years ago, a monk from India traveled to China. He began teaching people special movements to train the mind and body. His students learned to sit very still for a long time, breathing slowly. They learned shadow boxing and hand movements. All these movements came to be called kung-fu.

When a Japanese army invaded a Chinese island, kung-fu experts came to the rescue. They turned back the spears of the Japanese with their bare hands. The amazed Japanese called this weapon *kara* (empty) *te* (hand). Some Japanese then learned karate themselves, keeping it a secret for centuries. But after World War II, American soldiers discovered karate. The secret was no longer a secret. Teachers opened schools for people wanting to learn this ancient art. Today karate schools are all over the world.

_____ **1.** A monk came from India to
- **A.** China
- **B.** Japan
- **C.** America
- **D.** an island

_____ **2.** Kung-fu is a group of
- **A.** boxers
- **B.** bodies
- **C.** movements
- **D.** students

_____ **3.** Kung-fu experts turned back the
- **A.** secrets
- **B.** spears
- **C.** movements
- **D.** islands

_____ **4.** *Karate* is a
- **A.** Chinese word
- **B.** American word
- **C.** Indian word
- **D.** Japanese word

_____ **5.** Now karate schools are
- **A.** for fighters
- **B.** in Japan
- **C.** for strong hands
- **D.** all over the world

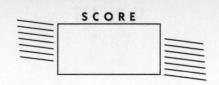
Karate is excellent exercise. It is also a fine means of self-defense. Pupils learn more than fifty ways to throw off attackers. They learn to strike the forty vital points of the body to defend themselves.

Students spend three months just learning how to stretch, squat, sit, jump, and turn. They learn to kick forward and backward as high as an attacker's chin. Students also learn the art of complete stillness. For ten minutes of each hour, they kneel quietly. They think peaceful thoughts. This part is often the hardest to learn.

The black belt is the highest award a karate student can earn. There are nine other levels of black belt beyond the first one. Very few karate champions have ever gone beyond the first.

6. Karate students learn how to
   A. find attackers            C. score forty points
   B. defend themselves         D. improve their nerves

7. During the first three months, students learn how to
   A. stun people               C. kick backward
   B. win belts                 D. lie down

8. One of the hardest lessons is learning how to
   A. jump and turn             C. stretch and sit
   B. drop the class            D. kneel quietly

9. The black belt is
   A. the highest award         C. sometimes too big
   B. the lowest award          D. easy to earn

10. Few karate champions
    A. sit quietly              C. jump backward
    B. win ten levels           D. concentrate well

Stargazing takes imagination. People who love stargazing see the stars as shining spots in a dot-to-dot drawing game. They imagine lines that connect groups of stars called constellations. A constellation is a group of stars that look like a person, an animal, or an object.

The constellation Orion is known as the hunter, after a hero from ancient Greek myths. To find Orion, first find the Big Dipper. The Big Dipper looks like a huge cup with a long handle. After you find the Big Dipper, turn around. There's Orion! He is outlined by four bright stars that form two triangles. The tips of the triangles seem to come together. Where they meet, there are three more bright stars. These form Orion's belt. Some fainter stars hang from the belt. These are Orion's sword.

_____ 1. When looking at a constellation, people try to imagine
   A. lines            C. spots
   B. games            D. groups

_____ 2. Groups of stars are called
   A. stargazers       C. constellations
   B. ancient myths    D. connections

_____ 3. Orion is named after a Greek
   A. object           C. animal
   B. story            D. hero

_____ 4. The four bright stars in Orion form
   A. a big cup        C. a long handle
   B. two triangles    D. an animal

_____ 5. Three bright stars form Orion's
   A. shoulder         C. belt
   B. sword            D. spear

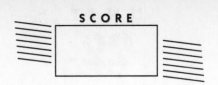
Different kinds of stars are in the constellation Orion. The star Betelgeuse makes Orion's right shoulder. *Betelgeuse* is an Arabic word that means "shoulder of the giant." The star itself is so huge that it is called a supergiant. Its diameter is four hundred times greater than that of our sun. Betelgeuse is considered a cool star. It is probably not as hot as our sun.

Rigel is the star that makes Orion's left foot. *Rigel* is the Arabic word for *foot*. Rigel is much brighter than Betelgeuse because it is much hotter. It's more than three times as hot as our sun. However, Rigel is just a baby in size compared to Betelgeuse.

A large, misty area near Orion's sword is called a nebula. It is a mass of shining gas and dust. The gases whirl together and may form new stars. As the new stars begin to shine, Orion will be brighter than ever.

---

_____ **6.** Betelgeuse makes
    **A.** Arabic words    **C.** different stars
    **B.** Orion's shoulder    **D.** huge sizes

_____ **7.** Betelgeuse is much larger than
    **A.** our sun    **C.** a diameter
    **B.** a supergiant    **D.** any nebula

_____ **8.** Rigel is brighter because it is
    **A.** bigger    **C.** hotter
    **B.** smaller    **D.** cooler

_____ **9.** Near Orion's sword is
    **A.** a cool star    **C.** a new star
    **B.** strange material    **D.** a nebula

_____ **10.** Orion may shine brighter
    **A.** when Rigel explodes    **C.** as dust shines
    **B.** as new stars shine    **D.** as dust forms

It was 5:00 in the morning on April 18, 1906. The city of San Francisco was sleeping. At 5:13 an earthquake shattered the peace. The ground shifted, and streets buckled. Water and sewer pipes broke apart. Buildings crumbled.

Two smaller earthquakes quickly followed. The city's electrical wires fell. The broken, sputtering wires set off a fire that devoured the city. Screaming people ran to the parks and the bay to escape the fire.

San Francisco's six hundred firefighters went into action. But they could not fill their hoses from the broken water pipes. The only water was in San Francisco Bay. Soon even this water was not enough. The fire reached the city's gas house. It exploded, becoming a gigantic fireball. Flames joined flames. The firefighters almost lost all hope.

_____ **1.** The earthquake hit San Francisco in the early
    **A.** afternoon      **C.** morning
    **B.** evening      **D.** night

_____ **2.** The fire was set off by
    **A.** broken sewer pipes      **C.** crumbled buildings
    **B.** fallen wires      **D.** the gas house

_____ **3.** People ran to the parks to find
    **A.** safety      **C.** buildings
    **B.** hoses      **D.** action

_____ **4.** The firefighters could only use water from
    **A.** water pipes      **C.** fire engines
    **B.** the bay      **D.** the gas house

_____ **5.** The firefighters almost lost hope when the
    **A.** pipes broke      **C.** wires fell
    **B.** gas house exploded      **D.** people screamed

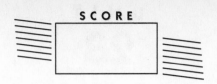
The firefighters tried to stop the fire by making a firebreak, a cleared strip of land. They used dynamite to knock down a long row of buildings, hoping the fire would die out when it reached the cleared land. But this firebreak did not work.

For two days the fire raged. On April 20 the firefighters used cannons to make a much larger firebreak. They flattened beautiful homes along Van Ness Avenue. The cannon shells dug a ditch five hundred feet wide and almost a mile long. But high winds helped the flames leap over the huge ditch. More cannons were fired, and more mansions fell. Finally the fire was stopped. In three days, more than twenty-five thousand buildings and five square miles of the city had been destroyed. Over seven hundred people lost their lives.

On April 21 a soft rain fell. The hot ashes cooled, and the citizens of San Francisco began to rebuild.

---

       **6.** A firebreak is made by
          **A.** stopping the fire   **C.** using water hoses
          **B.** clearing the land   **D.** calling firefighters

       **7.** The firefighters made the first firebreak by using
          **A.** buildings       **C.** strips
          **B.** dynamite      **D.** ditches

       **8.** Buildings on Van Ness Avenue were destroyed by
          **A.** raging fire     **C.** cannon shells
          **B.** high winds    **D.** hot ashes

       **9.** When the fire came to the second firebreak, it
          **A.** exploded      **C.** did not burn
          **B.** died out      **D.** jumped a ditch

       **10.** The fire lasted
          **A.** weeks        **C.** hours
          **B.** months      **D.** days

When Ludwig van Beethoven was 28 years old, he wrote a letter to a friend. "Do not tell anyone I am losing my hearing," wrote Beethoven. "Each day it grows worse. I notice the hearing loss most when I am with people. I cannot hear what they are saying, so I cannot answer them. I fear that people think I am unfriendly."

This letter was written in 1801. By that time Beethoven already had composed music for the piano and for small groups of instruments. He also had finished his first symphony. A symphony is a long piece of music for a full orchestra.

In spite of his growing deafness, Beethoven continued to write lovely music. For many years, he even conducted orchestras. However, by the year 1822, his hearing was gone. But this did not stop him from composing. Much of his best music was written after he could no longer hear at all.

_____ **1.** Beethoven's letter told about losing his
    **A.** music     **C.** secret
    **B.** hearing     **D.** friendships

_____ **2.** By 1801 Beethoven had already
    **A.** written much music     **C.** given up conducting
    **B.** become totally deaf     **D.** sent more letters

_____ **3.** Symphonies are played by
    **A.** pianos     **C.** small groups
    **B.** full orchestras     **D.** one instrument

_____ **4.** After 1822 Beethoven could no longer
    **A.** compose     **C.** write
    **B.** sing     **D.** hear

_____ **5.** Beethoven wrote much of his best music after he
    **A.** wrote symphonies     **C.** conducted people
    **B.** wrote letters     **D.** could not hear

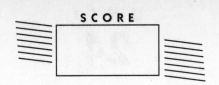
How could a deaf musician continue to create such fine work? The answer probably is that Beethoven could always hear the music in his head. Then he wrote down what he heard.

Beethoven kept to a strict schedule. He got up at dawn and wrote music until late afternoon. Now and then he walked in his garden and thought about his compositions. He never let anyone see his symphonies until they were completed.

Beethoven tried out his written piano pieces as he worked on them. He had his piano changed so that it played very loudly. He also used a special stick. He held one end of the stick in his mouth and rested the other end on the piano strings. As he touched the piano keys with his fingers, he could feel the strong vibrations made by the strings. The vibrations were carried along the stick. This way, Beethoven *felt* the beautiful music that he could hear only in his mind.

_____  **6.** Beethoven wrote music that he heard
      **A.** in a garden       **C.** in his mind
      **B.** with other people       **D.** in the morning

_____  **7.** Beethoven took walks and
      **A.** picked flowers       **C.** thought about music
      **B.** kept a diary       **D.** hid his symphonies

_____  **8.** The musician touched the keys of the piano with
      **A.** his hands       **C.** a stick
      **B.** his mouth       **D.** a string

_____  **9.** The stick allowed Beethoven to
      **A.** play loudly       **C.** fix pianos
      **B.** feel music       **D.** write better

_____  **10.** Beethoven used the stick
      **A.** when walking       **C.** to scare dogs
      **B.** to feel vibrations       **D.** to keep time

In the city of Metropolis, Illinois, there's a place called Superman Square. Comic book fans know why Metropolis honors Superman. In comic book stories, Superman lives in a city that is also called Metropolis.

Superman uses the name Clark Kent and pretends to be a reporter. Other superheroes also use disguises. Does Hal Jordan just work as a test pilot? No, he doesn't. He's also the Green Lantern. Peter Parker goes to college and writes for a newspaper. But Parker is also Spiderman. Bruce Wayne lives a fine life in his mansion. No one knows that this rich man is really Batman! Quiet Dr. Banner turns into the Hulk when he gets upset. This green giant battles evil people. When he has won, he becomes gentle Dr. Banner again. Superheroes do what we all would *like* to do. They fight evil with special strengths.

_____ **1.** Superman Square is
  A. a game            C. in a comic book
  B. part of a story   D. in a real city

_____ **2.** Hal Jordan is a
  A. pilot             C. college student
  B. rich man          D. reporter

_____ **3.** Peter Parker and Clark Kent both work
  A. as pilots         C. for a newspaper
  B. in mansions       D. in Metropolis

_____ **4.** The Hulk turns back into Dr. Banner when he
  A. eats spinach      C. has won
  B. becomes quiet     D. gains weight

_____ **5.** The Hulk battles people who are
  A. strong            C. green
  B. evil              D. upset

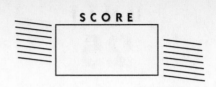
Charles Moulton created a cartoon character named Wonder Woman. Wonder Woman has special bracelets that keep her safe. She also has a golden lasso. She can capture people with it. Then they must follow her commands. Of course Wonder Woman has a disguise, too. She calls herself Diana Prince, and she works for the government.

Each superhero has special enemies. Wonder Woman chases spies. Batman fights The Joker and Penguin. The Hulk battles Tyrannus, a strange creature who can turn into a flame. One of Superman's main enemies is Mr. Mxyzlptlk. If you can say his name backwards, he will disappear!

Popeye gets his power in a funny way. When he eats spinach, his muscles grow. Spinach farmers in Crystal City, Texas, built a statue in his honor.

_____ **6.** Charles Moulton created
  **A.** The Joker      **C.** Diana Prince
  **B.** Tyrannus       **D.** Penguin

_____ **7.** The golden lasso makes people
  **A.** stay safe      **C.** catch things
  **B.** obey orders    **D.** wear bracelets

_____ **8.** Penguin and The Joker are
  **A.** special disguises   **C.** Batman's enemies
  **B.** new superheroes     **D.** government spies

_____ **9.** One enemy will disappear if you can
  **A.** turn into a flame   **C.** win against Sinestro
  **B.** capture Mars        **D.** say something special

_____ **10.** Popeye is popular in Crystal City because he
  **A.** enjoys spinach   **C.** works on a farm
  **B.** saves friends    **D.** lives in Texas

A baby girl named Atalanta was born to parents who did not want her, so they left her in the cold forest. A mother bear found her and taught her about the animals around her. As she grew, Atalanta learned to run swiftly, fight bravely, and live on her own.

One day Atalanta met some hunters who were amazed at her beauty and strength. They asked her to join them in an important task. A fierce animal called the Calydonian boar was destroying towns and terrifying everyone. King Oeneus had sent men out to kill the animal. But the boar killed every hunter who approached it.

Atalanta was not afraid of boars. She had seen them often in the woods. When she and the other hunters found the Calydonian boar, they surrounded it. The men shivered with fear. But Atalanta took out her bow, aimed her arrow, and killed the boar.

_____ **1.** Atalanta's parents did not
- A. need her
- B. want her
- C. find her
- D. leave her

_____ **2.** The baby was found by a
- A. boar
- B. hunter
- C. bear
- D. woman

_____ **3.** King Oeneus sent the men to
- A. find Atalanta
- B. roam the country
- C. go to the woods
- D. kill a beast

_____ **4.** The hunters were amazed at Atalanta's
- A. speed
- B. strength
- C. amazement
- D. importance

_____ **5.** Atalanta killed
- A. the hunters
- B. the bear
- C. the boar
- D. an arrow

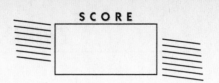
Atalanta found her parents. They were happy to have her back, but her father wanted her to get married. Atalanta felt that any man she married should be able to run as fast as she could. "Listen," said her father. "There are many men who want to marry you. Surely one of them can beat you in a race. That man will become your husband." So, to please her father, Atalanta agreed to run a series of races. But time and time again, the men lost.

Then it was Melanion's turn. He had three apples of pure gold, which he decided to use in his race. Atalanta and Melanion raced around the track. Each time Atalanta began to pass him, Melanion threw a golden apple to the side. Each time, Atalanta stopped to pick up the lovely thing. But she soon caught up with Melanion. The finish line was in sight as the racers ran side by side. Melanion tossed the third apple. As Atalanta paused to get it, Melanion panted across the line. Atalanta lost the race, but she won a husband as clever as she was.

_____ 6. Atalanta wanted to find
    A. a husband     C. a racer
    B. her home     D. her parents

_____ 7. Atalanta agreed to race to
    A. show off her skill    C. find an apple
    B. please her father    D. win a prize

_____ 8. Melanion had apples that were
    A. golden     C. thrown
    B. secret     D. swift

_____ 9. Atalanta stopped to
    A. lose races     C. pick up apples
    B. watch runners     D. help Melanion

_____ 10. Melanion won by being
    A. fast     C. handsome
    B. greedy     D. clever

# *Think and Apply*

## *Fact Finding*

Study the following index from a book about computers. Then use the facts listed to answer the questions.

---

**Index**

careers 110–119

commands 23, 30–31, 44–48

future applications 120–130

graphics 78–81

hardware 9–21

    CPU (Central Processing Unit) 10–13

    disk drive 18–20

    keyboard 17

    monitor or CRT (Cathode Ray Tube) 14–16

    printer 21

languages 50–55

software 22–24, 81, 92

word processing 85–92

---

1. You want to find out how computers will be used in the future.

   On which pages will you look? _____

2. How many pages are about graphics? _____

3. What subject is covered on pages 9 through 21? _____

   _____

4. You are interested in a job working with computers. On which

   pages will you look? _____

5. You want to find facts about word-processing software. On

   which page will you look? _____

**To check your answers, turn to page 62.**

## Listing Facts

List at least three facts you need to know in order to complete each task.

**A.** Do a science experiment.

1. _____

2. _____

3. _____

**B.** Apply for a job.

1. _____

2. _____

3. _____

**C.** Take a trip to a foreign country.

1. _____

2. _____

3. _____

**D.** Vote in an election.

1. _____

2. _____

3. _____

**E.** Throw a surprise birthday party for a friend.

1. _____

2. _____

3. _____

## *Facts Make a Difference*

   Pretend that you are writing a letter to the editor of a newspaper. You are concerned about litter in your area. Try to get people to help solve the problem. Include facts about the problem.

_____

_____

_____

_____

_____

_____

_____

_____

_____

_____

_____

_____

_____

_____

_____

_____

_____

_____

| *Unit 1* pp. 6-7 | *Unit 2* pp. 8-9 | *Unit 3* pp. 10-11 | *Unit 4* pp. 12-13 | *Unit 5* pp. 14-15 | *Unit 6* pp. 16-17 | *Unit 7* pp. 18-19 | *Unit 8* pp. 20-21 |
|---|---|---|---|---|---|---|---|
| | | | 11-22 | 11-28 | 12-13 | 12-13 | 12-21 |
| 1. B | 1. C | 1. B | 1. C | 1. C | 1. D | 1. D | 1. B |
| 2. C | 2. A | 2. D | 2. A | 2. B | 2. B | 2. B | 2. C |
| 3. A | 3. C | 3. A | 3. D | 3. D | 3. D | 3. A | 3. C |
| 4. C | 4. B | 4. C | 4. A | 4. C | 4. A | 4. C | 4. A |
| 5. D | 5. D | 5. A | 5. D | 5. B | 5. C | 5. A | 5. C |
| 6. B | 6. B | 6. C | 6. B | 6. D | 6. D | 6. D | 6. D |
| 7. A | 7. A | 7. B | 7. B | 7. A | 7. B | 7. C | 7. A |
| 8. C | 8. B | 8. D | 8. C | 8. B | 8. C | 8. A | 8. B |
| 9. A | 9. A | 9. C | 9. B | 9. B | 9. B | 9. C | 9. A |
| 10. D | 10. C | 10. A | 10. D | 10. C | 10. A | 10. C | 10. C |

レー |

| Unit 9 pp. 22-23 | Unit 10 pp. 24-25 | Unit 11 pp. 26-27 | Unit 12 pp. 28-29 | Unit 13 pp. 30-31 | Unit 14 pp. 32-33 | Unit 15 pp. 34-35 | Unit 16 pp. 36-37 |
|---|---|---|---|---|---|---|---|
| 1. C | 1. C | 1. D | 1. C | 1. B | 1. C | 1. A | 1. A |
| 2. B | 2. D | 2. D | 2. A | 2. A | 2. A | 2. D | 2. A |
| 3. C | 3. A | 3. B | 3. B | 3. B | 3. A | 3. A | 3. B |
| 4. D | 4. C | 4. B | 4. A | 4. C | 4. A | 4. B | 4. D |
| 5. A | 5. C | 5. A | 5. B | 5. C | 5. C | 5. C | 5. D |
| 6. C | 6. B | 6. C | 6. D | 6. A | 6. C | 6. D | 6. B |
| 7. A | 7. C | 7. C | 7. A | 7. A | 7. B | 7. A | 7. A |
| 8. C | 8. D | 8. D | 8. C | 8. B | 8. D | 8. B | 8. C |
| 9. B | 9. B | 9. B | 9. A | 9. A | 9. C | 9. B | 9. C |
| 10. C | 10. C | 10. A | 10. B | 10. D | 10. B | 10. C | 10. C |

| *Unit* **17**<br>pp. 38-39 | *Unit* **18**<br>pp. 40-41 | *Unit* **19**<br>pp. 42-43 | *Unit* **20**<br>pp. 44-45 | *Unit* **21**<br>pp. 46-47 | *Unit* **22**<br>pp. 48-49 | *Unit* **23**<br>pp. 50-51 | *Unit* **24**<br>pp. 52-53 | *Unit* **25**<br>pp. 54-55 |
|---|---|---|---|---|---|---|---|---|
| 1. D | 1. C | 1. D | 1. A | 1. A | 1. C | 1. B | 1. D | 1. B |
| 2. C | 2. B | 2. B | 2. C | 2. C | 2. B | 2. A | 2. A | 2. C |
| 3. A | 3. A | 3. A | 3. B | 3. D | 3. A | 3. B | 3. C | 3. D |
| 4. D | 4. D | 4. D | 4. D | 4. B | 4. B | 4. D | 4. C | 4. B |
| 5. B | 5. B | 5. A | 5. D | 5. C | 5. B | 5. D | 5. B | 5. C |
| 6. B | 6. D | 6. B | 6. B | 6. B | 6. B | 6. C | 6. C | 6. D |
| 7. A | 7. A | 7. A | 7. C | 7. A | 7. B | 7. C | 7. B | 7. B |
| 8. C | 8. C | 8. D | 8. D | 8. C | 8. C | 8. A | 8. C | 8. A |
| 9. C | 9. B | 9. D | 9. A | 9. D | 9. D | 9. B | 9. D | 9. C |
| 10. D | 10. B | 10. C | 10. B | 10. B | 10. D | 10. B | 10. A | 10. D |

## What are Facts? Page 2

*Fact*: December 1903

*Fact*: Orville Wright

## Practice Finding Facts, Page 3

**3.** B

## Fact Finding, Page 56

**1.** pages 120–130

**2.** four pages

**3.** hardware

**4.** pages 110–119

**5.** page 92

## Listing Facts, Page 57

Answers will vary.

## Facts Make a Difference, Page 58

Answers will vary.